Google
The Reading Dog

Sandy Childs

2QT Limited (Publishing)

First edition published 2019
2QT Limited (Publishing)
www.2QT.co.uk

Cover design and Illustrations by Joan Aitchison
Typesetting by Dale Rennard

Printed in Great Britain by
Lightning Source UK Ltd.

A CIP catalogue record for this book is available
from the British Library

ISBN 978-1-912014-30-9

All profits from the sale of this book will be donated to The Kennel Club Educational
Trust, Bark and Read Foundation (Registered Charity No. 1121454)

Foreword

This book is for anyone who works with, or has, children. It tells the story of Google (Mr Bear), a Golden Retriever who worked in school for eight years and saw - and helped - more than 25,000 young people.

The intention of Google The Reading Dog is to demonstrate how the love of a dog and its use in a learning context can enhance a young person's motivation and confidence to learn. Whether that young person is at nursery, primary or secondary school, is aged three or sixteen, has a special educational or emotional need, a dog like Google can provide positive reinforcement.

Although the book suggests ways in which working with Google could be used to support the school curriculum, it is not designed as an educational tool to measure levels of progress.

> 'He has four legs, with eyes like chocolate buttons, that melt when they look at you ... whose nose is like a wet pebble, with ears as soft as silk and fur golden like the sun ... His tail sways like wheat in the field and paws as big as bear's ... whose character is gentle, calm, helpful, intelligent, caring, loving and serene.'

These are just some of the metaphors that reluctant writers used to describe Google during his literacy project.

Acknowledgements

I need to say thank you to several people; without them, Google's legacy would have been very different.

- Sue Warrington, ex-head teacher, who championed us and has written part of this introduction and selected the stories

- Joan Aitchison, for stepping in and creating the beautiful illustrations

- The children who have allowed me to share their stories

- Eve Sticker, my old boss, who allowed my dog and me to go into schools

- Dog AID (Assistance in Disability), who supported us

- Holly-Anna Valavanis, for looking after Google's website

- The Kennel Club Educational Trust, Bark and Read Foundation, for providing financial support to develop the website and covering the costs so that no one had to pay to use them.

The biggest thank you goes to Chris Mancini who socialised and gave me Google. Google was bred initially as an assistance dog but was failed due to scurfy skin (dandruff). He had the best training and start in life, all shared with his best friend, Taggie.

Google not only changed my life but the lives of all the young people he met throughout his eight years in school.

Google

Name: Google

Kennel Club name: Mr Tom

Nickname: Mr Bear

Breed: Golden Retriever

Born: 09/04/2007

Qualifications: Demonstration Assistance Dog - Dog AID; Therapy Dog

Job: Teacher, model, TV and theatre star

Hobbies: Reading, swimming

Favourite food: Ice cream

Favourite toy: Tango

Favourite book: The Great Dog Bottom Swap by Peter Benchley

Favourite song: 'What I Am' (Will.I.Am)

Google's story

I am Sandy, a teacher for thirty-three years. I was honoured and privileged to have Google in my life and to be able to share him with others.

I started as a PE teacher in a secondary school before embarking on my career in special educational needs. I returned to mainstream education for the last eighteen years, working with pupils with special needs, mainly behavioural issues.

All teachers are hardworking and dedicated. They spend unseen hours outside the classroom, marking, planning and developing resources, trying to make learning interesting and engaging. It is hard work - unless you are lucky enough to have a teaching resource so special you just sit back and watch. When Google was in the room, 'remarkable things happened'.

 He motivated the unmotivated.

 He inspired those who didn't want to try to have a go.

 He gave confidence to the quiet, shy and lonely.

 He calmed the angry.

 He gave a voice to the selective mute.

 He gave light to the partially sighted.

 He helped overcome fears.

 He comforted the bereaved.

 He made the frightened feel safe.

As an assistance dog, Google represented the charity Dog AID. In assemblies, with his assistance dog skills, he showed how dogs can help people by picking up dropped things, taking off a coat and socks, answering - well, getting - the phone, putting his toys away.

He liked to show off his tricks, like dunking the basketball and playing quoits. He loved the attention and applause, which he shared with his favourite toy, Tango.

He impressed everyone he met, especially with his reading. He filled assemblies with customary non-attenders because 'there is a dog that can read'. No one believed it, so they came to see for themselves.

This was so inspirational to everyone that Google's Literacy Project was born with the help of an ex-colleague and friend Lindy Jones, author of *The Voice in My Head is Perfect*. Initially Lindy accompanied us to the sessions as an English teacher until she was forced into early retirement having been diagnosed with Motor Neurone Disease. With Google's support, she felt confident enough to go into school for two more years. Google and I carried on the work when sadly she was taken from us.

I could go on forever about how wonderful he was. This book is a small selection of stories written by young people who either struggled to read and write, lacked the confidence to try, or had other emotional difficulties. The grammar and spelling may not have been perfect but that didn't matter. What mattered was that they finished a story and then had the confidence, with Google by their side, to read it to other primary school children. It was the beginning of their journey.

About Google
by Sue Warrington, former head teacher

'A dog that can read?' You have to see it to believe it. I've had the privilege of watching Google read and, better still, inspire reluctant readers to begin that adventure.

To find out about Google, you only need to read the children's stories written during sessions with him - he was a rascal, fun-loving and clever. He was a learner, able to learn from his mistakes. Above all, he was a good, loyal friend. He motivated students to develop their literacy skills, build their confidence and develop their emotional intelligence.

Remarkable things happened when Sandy brought Google to a classroom. He created a magical experience in a calm, safe place where vulnerable young people could feel they belonged and build a special bond with him.

One of my many Google memories is of an overnight camping trip with 200 Year 7s. A forlorn boy was sitting glued to the staff, feeling overwhelmed and homesick - should we phone home and end his misery? Enter Sandy and Google. Sandy asked the boy to hold

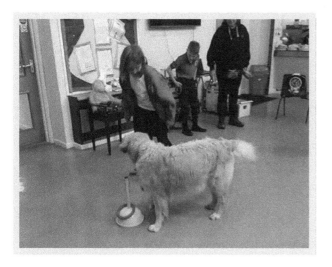

Google's lead and maybe take him for a walk. Moments later the boy was grinning and, like the Pied Piper, was followed by loads of other Year 7s asking questions about Google and hoping to hold his lead too. The boy had a great weekend, made many new friends and thrived on his journey through school. Serendipity and Google magic!

Thank you, Google, for unlocking learning for so many young people who were lucky to have worked with you.

Google the teacher

The impact that animals have on children (and adults) cannot be overestimated. It is difficult to put into words and must be seen to be believed if you don't know dogs. Google is very calm and even children who are normally quite disruptive tend to be calm around him.

- The mute girl who could speak to Google. The girl who spoke with a strange voice talked normally to him. He only had to wag his tail.

- The boy who couldn't sit still and had difficulty sleeping could lie on the floor with Google, who put his paws on him, licked his hands and helped him to sleep.

- The boy in an EBD (Emotional, Behavioural Disorders) school who had 2:1 support and was not part of any groups engaged with Google for thirty minutes, watching him do his tricks and getting him to do some for him. More surprisingly, he then took Google's soft toy back to the headteacher and had his first ever conversation with her about what Google had done. He was in Year 9 and had been in the school since primary age!

- The poorly behaved class that wanted to watch Google and work with him. They knew he didn't like shouting or he wouldn't perform. They watched quietly and contentedly and took turns.

One of my most abiding memories of Google's power was at a school for individuals with emotional behaviour difficulties. It was our second visit; we had been to assembly the first time, but the school wanted him to go again. I asked the headteacher if I could get a young person to take Tango, Google's favourite toy, and hide him outside so Google could find him.

Everyone in the school bundled out and watched him search for Tango; they wanted to see it again and again. All day I heard staff saying, 'The whole school going in and out, and no incidents.' Eventually, at the end of the day when we were taking a young man back to the head after a session with Google, I asked what this meant.

The head teacher said, 'During assembly the whole school went outside, unplanned and came back in - and there was not one incident. It's unheard off.'

I hadn't even thought about it, such was my belief in the awesome ability of my dog to captivate his audience. Not only that, but every one of the students wrote stories about him and many read them out. This was our second visit. Three weeks earlier we had done the first lesson of the literacy project; the staff then did the other five. When we went back to listen to them and their stories, we noticed that the students remained motivated.

These are just some of the examples I have witnessed when working with Google and young people.

There was a total disbelief on their faces as he did the action relating to a word on a flash card, e.g. sit, down, stand, cross paws.... or any of the twelve words he could read. The activity was very inspirational and motivational. I said to the children, 'If a dog can do all that, what can you do?'

He went around the class making sure no-one felt left out. His intuition told him not to go to the child who was nervous or unsure but to keep his distance. He had real emotional intelligence and picked up on people who were upset. In all the years we worked together in schools, every child had stroked him by the end of his visit. 'I liked the way Google made everyone happy - and he liked an audience, too.'

One of the things I often heard was, 'I don't really like dogs, but I like you.' Google would look at them and slowly wag his tail.

A lot of theory has been written about the impact that dogs can have but none of it can compare to watching the interaction between Google and the young people with whom he came into contact.

In the words of one headteacher: 'When Google is in the room remarkable things happen.'

Dogs in School

While the concept of taking dogs into school to assist learning is not a new idea, it seems to have become increasingly popular of late. I wish every school could have a dog like Google that visits.

There is no doubt that animals - and dogs in particular because of their sociability - can have a positive impact on young people.

Google was bred as an assistance dog and his training complimented this. His calm demeanour was rarely ruffled.

'I had to break up a very physical fight with some Year 11 boys who were throwing chairs. Google stood by. He decided the most important thing he could do was lean against and push a heavily pregnant colleague into the safety of an office and put his head on her knee.'

Whole playgrounds would run to him. His name was chanted out of the windows as he walked in: 'Goooogle.' He was screamed at by those frightened of dogs. He never once broke stride.

Increasingly I am being asked my advice about taking dogs into schools, including getting a particular breed of puppy specifically for this task. Schools are volatile, noisy, crowded, unpredictable places. You must be absolutely sure your dog can cope; this type of interaction is not right for all dogs.

Their temperament must be right, their training is essential, and therefore an assessment needs to be undertaken. Every step must be taken to ensure the dog's wellbeing because they haven't chosen to be there.

Taking a dog into schools is different from taking one in for visits and not all dogs can cope with a mainstream school environment. A school dog becomes a *'working dog'*. Careful consideration ***must be*** given as to whether a *'pet dog'* has the breeding and training that would make them suitable for this role.

Bark & Read

The Kennel Club's Bark & Read project, supported by the Kennel Club Educational Trust provides practical support to our partner service providers, big and small, to enable them to bring specially trained and assessed support dogs into classrooms and libraries to assist children and young people to become confident and happy readers.

Between them all, our partner service providers are bringing approximately 1500 dog and handler teams to 1500 schools in England, Wales, Scotland and Northern Ireland.

This idea is a very simple one, but the effect, both on reading levels and behaviour is really quite remarkable. Reading to and interacting with a classroom dog helps children and young people to love reading, overcome shyness and increase their confidence, and improve concentration and behaviour.

Reading to dogs is effective because of the calming effect the dogs' presence has on children and because the dog will listen to the children read without being judgemental or critical. This comforting environment helps to nurture children's enthusiasm for reading and provides them with the confidence needed to read aloud. During reading sessions, the child is able read comfortably and to make mistakes and be given the opportunity to self-correct at their own pace without feeling self-conscious. Doing so out loud encourages positive social behaviour, enhances self-esteem, motivates speech and inspires children to have fun and enjoy the experience of reading.

It is a very flexible programme, so it can be customised to suit a school's particular needs. All over the country, children are learning to love reading with the support of these amazing doggy companions.

You can find out more about Bark & Read, our service providers and Standards of Practice on our website www.thekennelclub.org.uk/barkandread

Enhancing learning opportunities
in school or at home

Using Google to motivate and inspire was not limited to activities related to English such as reading and writing. He also helped with:

Maths	Calculating distances and angles, e.g. how far is Tango away from Google; what is the shortest route for Google to reach Tango?
Science	Looking at a dog's sense of smell, their physiology, nutrition in dogs and humans
History	Dogs' roles in the past, particularly in World War 2
Learning to learn	How does Google learn?
Art	Life drawings
PE	Walking, running, jumping, rolling, swimming
Geography	Where did Google go for a walk? Using map references. Different breeds and where they are from
Music	Making music/adding rhythms to a story. Google's favourite book was going to be a musical; sadly he never got to see it being performed
English	Reading, writing

Google was used as a reward for good effort, work, attendance and behaviour. Check out Google's other book The Bear Bones of Behaviour

Learning out of school

The impact that a dog has is not limited to the work they do in schools. Any family that owns a dog has one of the best teaching resources available to help their child to learn and make it fun at the same time. All it needs is a bit of imagination.

The emotional intelligence Google possessed was exceptional; his intelligence was special. He made a difference to many by improving their confidence, motivation and communication skills. He gave them an opportunity to express their intelligence in a different way and showed them that how he learns is no different to the way that they do. Perhaps the biggest thing he did was to make learning fun and to help them learn to love being around dogs.

Google's Diary

This is an example of one of Google's diary, each one is based around a theme such as trust or respect. You can find more on the website

http://thebearbonesofeducation.org

Consequences

I was in the 'doghouse' on Tuesday evening. After I left C-School, I went to another school. The Headteacher wouldn't let me stay in the car as it was too hot, so I went into her office. She phoned her secretary to bring me a bowl of water, which she did. How important am I?

Anyway, Tuesday evening we went for a walk to Hillyfields. I like it there, but it makes me sad, as it was one of Nadia's favourite walks because she liked the water. I do miss her really, even though I don't have to share my ice cream.

I think all those nice things people said about my character being friendly, calm, clever and well-behaved went to my head. No one said I was naughty, mischievous or badly behaved, which I can be sometimes.

We met up with my friend, Bertie the Rottweiler, who I hadn't seen for ages, and two Labradors. Max kept stealing my ball and I can't remember the girl's name but she fancied me. I heard her owner say so, because she hadn't told me to get lost!

I rolled in fox poo!! I know it's horrible, but I am a boy after all! When Sandy smelled me, I can't tell you the names she called me - they were very rude! I know she doesn't really mean it because she loves me whatever, but I haven't done it for so long I forgot the consequences. When we got home, I got smeared with tomato sauce and vinegar. I smelled like a chip. Then I got soaked with cold water, then shampooed and rinsed again. Sandy was still swearing at me, but she got my dinner. I was afraid I might not get any! Just when she took my coat off, I thought it was all over and I had been forgiven but she then put this orange stuff on me to make me smell better. I smell like a girl - and then I got sprayed with something else too! I tell you, I'm not going to roll in fox poo again, ever - well, until the next time when I forget the consequences.

Wednesday

I go to agility on Wednesdays. Sometimes I like it and sometimes I can't be bothered. The lady that teaches me asks every week whether it's Google or his brother who has turned up. My brother is the good one. I always keep them guessing.

I like it apart from the weaves; I don't see the point of going in and out when I can go up the side.

When I do it right, I get ice cream, but not if I miss a pole or enter on the wrong side. I don't like the seesaw any more. I went up too slowly and scared myself as it tipped back, and I had to jump off. I can do it again really, but I get better rewards if they think I'm still scared!

Taggie has arthritis in her paw now, so she has had to retire. I don't know if she knows yet. Duffie is a beginner but he is a mad Collie so loves it and he is very fast.

They decided it was Google's brother who was at agility this week - so I got lots of ice cream! On Wednesday night I was a very good boy as a Muntjac jumped out in front of me and I didn't chase it. The same happened again on Thursday on the golf course and I didn't chase them either, there were two!

Friday

On Friday I went into school where I was the guest at bingo, which is being held as a fundraiser for the Dog Aid Charity for which I am an ambassador. I know C-School have ambassadors too, as I helped them make a DVD last year. It was fun and I wore a school tie - properly, as well. I thought I looked very smart.

At the weekend we didn't go away anywhere so I got a long lie in until 11am on Saturday, then had a lazy afternoon after a long walk. On Sunday we went to pick up two other Golden Retrievers. They got in my car, I wasn't happy. After our walk with Duffy and Roxie, they got back in my car and came home with me. That's all very well as they are Retrievers - but when Barley got Tango that was just too much! He is a few months younger than me and needs putting in his place. Then he played too rough with Heidi. She's nearly eleven and he should have more respect for his elders!

They are coming to stay for a week in August so I guess I'll just have to put up with them, but Barley need not think I'm going to put all my toys away when he gets them out. He'll have to learn to do that himself!

Selection of stories by children
who met and worked with Google

The Hot Day

Hello, my name is Google. Today is very hot day and I have had to drink a lot of water from my bowl.

The reason why I am so thirsty is because I had an adventure on the beach today with my friends Tango & Duffy. It all began this morning at 8am, we were just wandering around having fun, when Duffy said to me "Google look in the sea! I just saw a big monster!" I looked out to sea and saw the monster and realised that the monster needed help, he had a fishing hook in his mouth and was in a lot of pain.

I jumped into the sea and swam out to the monster. I told the monster not to panic that I was going to help him.

I grabbed the hook with my mouth and slowly pulled it out.

The Monster said thank you to me and told me that he would give me 1 wish, because he was a magic monster.

My wish was that more dogs could be trained like me to help more disabled people.

The Missing Ball

One day, Google and Duffie were bored. 'Duffie, I'm bored.' Google told Duffie. 'I have the same feeling Gooey.' Duffie responded with a sigh. Duffie likes calling Google with the nickname, 'Gooey' because he thinks it's funny. 'Why don't we go to the park to play a game?' asked Duffie. 'Might as well. I do need to get some exercise, Duffie.' Google told Duffie, ashamed. Duffie laughed at Google and his comment. 'I know! You are a bit chubby.' Duffie giggled. Google growled viciously and then barked loudly. 'Whoa! Sorry Google, I didn't know that wo.uld hurt your feelings. Your bark is like a lion's roar!' Duffie apologised to Google. 'It's OK. I can get annoyed easily.' Google said angrily. So Google and Duffie begged to Sandy to go to the park to play ball.

Fifty minutes later and they arrived at the park. As they told Sandy, they went to play with Google's only tennis ball. Duffie and Google played with the ball and Duffie got too excited. 'I got the ball Google! Catch!' Duffie shouted as he threw the ball with lots of power. The ball zoomed over

Google's head and Sandy had to duck to avoid being hit in the face by a tennis ball. The ball went flying away. It was lost! 'Oops! Sorry Google, for losing your only ball.' Duffie whined. 'It's OK Duffie. We can go to the beach and relax instead.' Sandy told to Duffie and Google when Goggle was crying. 'I guess we'll go to the beach then … ' Google howled sadly. So Google and Duffie hopped into Sandy's pink Limousine, with air conditioning on full blast (because the dogs were on board), and they went to the beach.

One hour later, Google, Duffie and Sandy got to the beach east from the park. Google and Duffie decided to have a race. Duffie won the race and Google went to sit on the sand. 'Hey, guys? Is it just me, or do you see the sun upon the sand?' Google questioned Duffie. 'I can see the sun! Yeah! You're right Google.' Duffie screamed joyfully. Sandy went to see this 'object' and came back to Google and Duffie. 'That's no sun!' Sandy exclaimed whilst cuddling Google and Duffie, 'It's the ball!' Google and Duffie barked joyfully and they played with the ball until it was time to go home. So they hopped back into Sandy's pink Limousine, with air conditioning on full blast (because the dogs were on board), and they went back home.

'What a tiring day!' sighed Google. He was weary. 'I agree, Google.' Duffie and Sandy both agreed. So Google, Duffie and Sandy comfortably climbed into their beds and they fell asleep. After ten minutes, Google opened one eye. 'Stop snoring Sandy … ' Google whispered to himself as he fell asleep.

I'm biased because I watched this vulnerable, lonely lad cut his own furrow through secondary school. He knew he was different from the crowd and he was isolated; that's why time with Google was calming, safe and special. The crowd envied him having Google time. He survived through GCSEs and Google played a part in helping to build his confidence.

The Story of How I Met Google

One spectacular sunny day, I got a call from a teacher saying I needed to go to a maths classroom. I thought I should run away and bury myself inside a box just at the thought of maths.

Anyway, I went along and as I opened the door I heard a howling noise going whoooh. I thought to myself that it sounded like a wolf.

However, when I went in to go and see what was in there, I soon realised it wasn't. Instead I saw it was him, my world superhero Google. As I went to stroke him, he jumped on me and gave me a huge hug. That's when I knew we were soul mates forever.

The End

I like this short and simple piece of writing which confirms the value of Google as a rich classroom resource. J's simile lurks in this piece of writing, reflecting the emphasis on developing literacy, but there's so much more here. The door to Maths may have closed but with Google's friendship a door opened for J.

All About Google

It was a hot sunny day. Google and Taggie went to the beach and swam together in the sea. They had lots of fun. They then lay in the sun to dry off. They were very tired and fell asleep.

However, Google was only pretending to be asleep. As soon as he saw that Taggie was asleep he decided to go on an adventure to find a bone that he had buried a long time ago.

When Google eventually found the bone, he ran quickly back to Taggie. He woke Taggie up and they played together with the bone.

The End

This reminds us of Google the rascal and all his energy, but again of the importance of friendship - what good's a bone without a friend to play with you?

Digging Competition

One Sunday afternoon, Google was feeling rather lonely, and then there was a bark at the door, 'Bark, Bark' it was Jeeves.

'Come on Google, let's go out and play!'

'I am glad you came, I was feeling so bored.'

'Good timing then, let's have a competition of who can dig the biggest hole.'

'Let's go!' said Google.

Jeeves ran ahead, he was much livelier than Google and Google struggled to keep up with him.

At last they reached the hills. They were covered with bright lemon yellow buttercups and small white daisies. The dogs had so much fun running through the flowers, chasing bees and butterflies.

'Right, you dig here and I'll dig over there' said Jeeves.

They each started digging up the grass into the dirt with their front paws. Soon all the dogs were covered with cocoa-brown dirt. Google started to bark madly. Jeeves ran over to see. Google had dug up a huge bone. He'd only dug some of it. Jeeves helped him dig around it and finally they both got the bone out.

'I guess we are both winners then' said cheeky Jeeves.

Google picked the bone up in his mouth. He could taste the delicious flavour of the ham. Holding it tightly in his mouth, they found a nice comfortable spot on the grass, lay down, and began gnawing on the bone. They sat there all day long and chewed the whole bone to bits. Google and Jeeves were very happy and spent the rest of the day, sleeping in the shade of an old willow tree.

A story which shows how the students were able to develop and extend their vocabulary in these lessons... 'covered in bright lemon buttercups and small white daisies ... running through the flowers chasing bees and butterflies'. And a competition ending with Jeeves and Google both as winners ... another good lesson for the students.

The Snowy Day

It had been snowing all night long. When Google woke up, he went outside and found everything carpeted in white fluffy snow. Google was a golden retriever and his fur was as bright as the sun. Google went outside and the snow covered his golden fur. The snow was deep and Google had to leap, rather than run. Taggie was already outside playing in the snow. When Taggie saw Google he ran up to him. They then ran around chasing each other, romping through the deep snow. Taggie made a snowball and threw it at Google's face. Taggie yelled, 'you got snowed!'

Suddenly a bark echoed through the snow, it was Duffie. Duffie barked, 'let's make a snowman.'

All three dogs, took turns to push around a ball of snow with their noses. They made two large balls of snow and pushed them on top of each other to make a snowman. Google ran home to get a scarf to wrap around the snowman's neck. Taggie snuck a carrot out of his house and stuck it into the snowman to make a nose. Duffie put small rocks in its head for eyes and a mouth. They then all ran around the snowman, playing and barking and played a game called DP, also known as Doggy Patrol.

Doggy patrol is a game where you have to look for things to play with. Taggie accidentally fell down a hole in the ground that was covered with snow. Google howled for his friends and said 'let's form a dog ladder.' All his friends came running and got Taggie out. By now they were almost frozen and exhausted. Luckily Sandy called them to come back indoors, where they sat in front of the fireplace with a cup of hot chocolate.

There's adventure, danger and rescue all wrapped up in J's story which engages the reader.

Play Fighting

Google and Duffie were play fighting in the freezing cold snow. It was so obvious that they were having a fantastic time. Google got his front paws out to high jump over Duffie, but slipped and Google fell on the floor straight away. Duffie was laughing his head off and rolling around on the floor, but poor Google was embarrassed. Duffie threw a snow ball at Google's face to try and make him laugh. Google's face was covered in snow.

Taggie came along and saw Google and Duffie play fighting in the snow, he watched them for a while but got jealous and started walking away. Google went to look for Taggie, he then spotted him crying and hiding behind the big oak tree that was covered in snow.

Google went over to speak to Taggie. 'Taggie why are you crying mate?' barked Google.

'I'm not crying.' said Taggie

'C'mon, don't be upset, you can play with us!'

Taggie asked what was on Google's face. Google said 'Oh! It's just snow, Duffie threw a snow ball at my face.'

'Ouch'

'What?'

'That must be very painful!'

'No it wasn't it was just a snowball!'

'No it must be painful because the snow must be very cold!'

'Come on let's all go and play all together before the snow melts.'

They started racing back to the field to see who could get their first. Taggie slipped on an icy patch and fell over. Google ran back to get help. Duffie panicked but Google calmed everyone down, as he knew what to do. Duffie whimpered and shivered from the cold. Google covered Duffie with a blanket and called for an ambulance. Taggie was taken to hospital to have an x-ray; he had broken his back legs. His paws had to be bandaged. Google and Duffie went to visit Taggie in hospital and brought him his favourite doggy biscuits.

'Duffie whimpered and shivered in the snow' but Google stays calm and saves the day.

The Adventure of the Lost Tango

The Adventure OF the Lost Tango.

Once there was a little cheeky dog called google he's smart tow. He has a brown nose like a choclate button, He has fur like a golden coin in a treasure chest. His eyes are like melted choclate. Google has a faborate toy called tango. He is orange and hairy with big beely eyes. One morning tango has gone! Google was terrified he burst into tears whats a matter google said sandy. Sandy is googles owner woof woof yove lost tango woof find him with tom woof. When Ton came he saw google was up set. Tom walked up to google whats amatter google I've lost Tango oh no lets search but he's no where how do you know because I've looked with sandy. Come on lets look more on! lets go. Oh look A map lets follow it because there's a picture of tango. Yaaa! lets go! oh look theres tango google I've missed you I've missed you too I wasn't that you said Tom dont think about saying bae! sorry its ok! Then they whent home by google by Tom oh you foun tango woof woof

The End
by
Anastacia Eve constantinou
xxx
xx
x

29

The Loch Ness Adventure

My name is Google, I am the clever one. One weekend, Sandy drove us to Scotland. We stayed in a small cottage by the Loch Ness Lake. I didn't roam around like Duffie and Taggie. I preferred to enjoy the tranquillity of the Scottish Moors.

Duffie and Taggie saw a large deer and they chased it right down to the loch. The deer got away but Duffie and Taggie dived nose first in to the loch. Luckily they managed to get out of the cold water and splashed water everywhere, including over me. Whilst they dried off, I told them the story about me and the Loch Ness monster.

A long, long time ago there was a legend about a monster that lived in a lake called Ness. It was rumored the monster was as big as a football pitch, with four eyes and liked to eat puppies. When I was just a puppy, I went on an adventure to explore the area around Loch Ness. I began throwing food in the loch to see if I could spot the monster. Suddenly I heard a roaring noise coming from the lake - it was the monster!! I started barking. The four-eyed head popped out of the water. I was very scared, but I stood quietly.

The monster asked: 'Aren't you frightened, little puppy?' I couldn't bark, but just shook my head.

Then the monster said, 'I like you. Everyone always runs away when they see me.'

'You don't eat puppies, do you?' I barked.

'Of course not' replied the monster in a gentle voice.

And that was how me and the Loch Ness monster ended up being friends.

A story within a story, with a great simile to describe Nessy for the reader. While the younger, more energetic dogs get themselves into trouble, clever Google wins through again by talking things through... I know a few adults/politicians who could learn from this!!

The World of Adventures of Google

Once upon a time, at Google's home, Google and Jeeves where bored.

Jeeves and Google went to ask Sandy if they could go to the beach and surf the biggest wave ever. Sandy said 'Yes' so they got ready to go; they got their sun glasses, surf board and a picnic basket full sandwiches for Sandy, doggy treats and ice cream (it was a special picnic basket with ice packs in it to keep the ice-cream frozen.)

On the way to the beach they went to a shop to pick up a red and white picnic blanket with doggy bones on it. It was as soft as a cloud - there's a simile there!!

When they arrived at the beach they chose a good place to have their picnic, near to the sea but away from the dangerous boulders. Then they had a snack, then it was time to surf the biggest waves in history!

After they had surfed the biggest waves in history they were as wet as rain (another simile!) Sandy said to Google and Jeeves 'What wet dogs you are!' she got a towel and dried Google and Jeeves off. After they got dried they had an ice-cream, chocolate ice-cream for Sandy, vanilla for Google and banana for Jeeves. They said 'Yumee - this is such good ice cream! Sandy, can we have some more?'

Sandy said 'No - you don't want to make a pig of yourself - we'll have some more later Google and Jeeves.'

After they had their ice-creams they packed their stuff up and moved up the beach...

Then they heard the clash of thunder and saw the flash of lightning. A fire had started on a fishing boat out at sea. Google and Jeeves said to Sandy 'FIRE, FIRE! Out on that boat.' Sandy dialled nine, nine, nine and the person who answered asked what service she needed. 'There's a fire on a boat on the sea, come quickly!' So the fire brigade sent their fire boat to put out the blaze.

Google, Sandy and Jeeves were thanked by the fire brigade for spotting the fire because they saved the lives of the people on the boat and the people of the oil tanker that was near the burning boat. They were made into honorary fire fighters and given a big, heavy, shiny medal.

The fire fighters were pleased with Google and Jeeves because their radar was broken because one of the circuits was fried because too much power had been rushing through it, so they hadn't spotted the burning boat.

After their long day they all went home and went to bed ready for the next day when they went up on the hillside. They were going to take some good photos of the countryside for a birthday card for one of their friends whose birthday was next week - Scooby was their name. But the fog was rolling in from the coast. It was as thick as pea soup - another simile.

Sandy said quickly before we get trapped in the fog and get lost - jump in the car. But Jeeves heard someone shouting 'HELP.' But Google was too worried about getting trapped in the fog to tell Sandy about someone shouting for help. And, Google wasn't paying attention. Sandy called 999. Again. She called the police to come and help find the missing person but Jeeves had already run off to help them. Google wasn't that far behind him, they were going like a flash - as fast as a light bulb turning on. The vanished into the fog like light bulbs being turned off on a dark night.

Sandy went running after them, she knew where they were because Google's leash was a noisy one and it made a rattling sound like a rattle snake. Sandy went running after the sound. She forgot her scarf but luckily enough the police brought their dog with them so the dog was able to follow Sandy by smell. But then they ran through a lake and the dog lost their scent. The mountain where the guy was stuck at was really tall and the part where the guy was was not foggy, and the guy had his leg stuck in between two stones. Google and Jeeves dug his leg out like a digger digging up gold. Soon he was free and he managed to get to the police safely because Google and Jeeves smelt another wet dog which was the police dog. He was as wet as the rain. Soon Sandy had caught up to Google and Jeeves and helped the guy walk because they thought he had a broken ankle.

The police gave Sandy, Jeeves and Google a medal again. A big shiny medal that was more shiny than gold. They gave Sandy. Google and Jeeves a tour around their police station and the keys to the police station.

THE END

...But the fog was rolling in from the coast. It was as thick as pea soup - another simile ... I liked A's cheeky aside - he clearly knows how to use similes - one of the learning objectives well and truly met!!!

CHARLIE'S CHRISTMAS ADVENTURE

It was a perfect day for sledging in the South Pole. Charlie the penguin and his best friend, Slippy the seal were enjoying going fast down the huge icy hills.

"This is so much fun" yelled Slippy.

"Let's go faster" Charlie cried with excitement.

BANG!!!

The two friends had crashed.

"Are you OK, Slippy?" Charlie asked rubbing his sore head.

"I'm fine but what was that we crashed into?" Slippy replied.

The two friends went for a closer look and there buried in the snow was...

A reindeer.

"Hello, is that you Mr Claus?" shouted the reindeer.

The two friends explained, "If you are looking for Santa you have come to the wrong place!"

Charlie informed the reindeer he was in the South Pole and Santa lived in the North pole.

WHOOPS!!!" sobbed the reindeer.

"I really need to get to the North Pole because Santa needs me to deliver presents" the sad reindeer told Charlie and Slippy.

"No problem, I will help you" Charlie reassured the reindeer.

The reindeer told Charlie his name was Loafa and he had been getting some exercise before Christmas Eve however he had got lost.

Charlie decided to asked his friend the Ocra for a lift to the North Pole. The new friends jumped on the Orca's back and set off on an amazing adventure.

However after a while the Orca, sadly cried "It's too hot I need to stop".

Loafa and Charlie jumped off the Orca onto land and waved goodbye.

The two friends walked and walked, but the hot sun kept beating down and down, making Loafa and Charlie warmer and warmer.

Suddenly Loafa spotted two other animals. He asked them "Is this the North Pole?"

"No" hissed the snake.

"This is the Sahara desert" the camel explained, "You need to carry on travelling north".

The two friends looked disappointed.

"It's far too hot and I can't walk another step" moaned Charlie.

"We could always fly" Loafa excitedly replied, "Santa's reindeer have magical powers, don't you know?"

With that the two friends waved goodbye and flew off.

"Watch out!" screeched Charlie.

However it was too late.

BOOM!!!

Loafa had crashed.

"What was that?" Loafa said puzzled.

"That is the Eiffel tower" a strange voice said. There standing next to the two friends was a pink poodle.

"Is this the north pole?" Loafa inquired.

Loafa and Charlie had landed in Paris and the two friends still had to travel further north.

Once again Loafa and Charlie waved goodbye to another new friend and carried on.

"Oh no!" Loafa suddenly shouted "look at the time" and he pointed to a big clock. It was almost Christmas Eve and Charlie and Loafa were still not at the North Pole.

"Where are we?" asked a confused Loafa.

"You are in London" answered a wise old owl.

"The Big Guy is going to be worried" a sad loafa added.

Charlie explained to the wise old owl the problem the two friends were in.

It was at this stage that the wise old owl came up with a solution, "just follow the North Star and you will be there in no time what so ever".

A pleased Loafa and Charlie said a massive thank you and waved goodbye.

"Look" yelled Charlie excitedly "It's the North Pole"

The two friends landed but there couldn't see Santa anywhere.

"ROAR!!!"

A giant polar bear came running over. Loafa and Charlie were extremely scared.

"Don't worry" another voice calmly said. It was a second polar who was a lot happier.

"Biff is in a bad mood because he thinks that Santa isn't going to bring him any presents", The nice cuddly polar bear laughed.

"It's not fair" the angry polar bear screamed.

Loafa then had a fantastic idea. He told the angry polar bear, if he helped the two friends find Santa, he would inform Santa what a good polar bear he had been".

"That's a deal", this brought a giant smile to the polar bear's face.

The now happy polar took the friends by the hand and started walking. After walking up and down some vast hills, over an icy lake and through a dark forest, the polar bear stopped and pointed, "Here you are".

Loafa started to jump up and down, "it's the big guy!!!" and he raced over to greet a pleased Santa.

"Just in time you silly reindeer" Santa laughed. "Are you ready to go?

"Yes, yes, yes, but can my new friend Charlie please come with us and help?

Santa agreed. So Santa, Loafa and Charlie delivered presents to all the good boys and girls (and polar bears) all around the world.

At the end of the busy day, Santa dropped Charlie back at the South Pole. Santa reached into his special sack and gave him a personal present. It was a snow globe and inside was an image of Santa, Loafa and Charlie.

"This is so you will always remember our adventure" Loafa said smiling.

"Thank you, this has been the best Christmas ever" a happy little penguin said.

HAPPY CHRISTMAS EVERYONE

The end

Postscript

It is with huge sadness but immense pride that this book has come together. Unfortunately, Google will be unable to take the final bow he so deserved after his retirement.

On Friday 29th June 2018, aged eleven, Google was taken over the rainbow bridge, far too soon.

He was my best friend, my soulmate, my once-in-a-lifetime companion who taught me so much. It was my privilege to have him in my life and to be able to share him with others.

I think it is only fitting that the final words are from a young man of seven years of age who only ever met Google twice. He was describing this picture I had posted on Facebook that his mother had shown him.

Thank you, Google Bear - those you met will never forget you.

'Google was so special the clouds drew his picture because he is in the sky now.'

Visit Google's website

www.thebearbonesofeducation.org

and follow on Facebook

 Google Bear

Gallery

CPSIA information can be obtained
at www.ICGtesting.com
Printed in the USA
BVHW021720070219
539733BV00022B/720/P